365 Days of Things Ever Said

Finding Inspiration, Leadership, and Change in Life and Work

MAX WINTERS

myfinaladviser.com

DISCLAIMER: While all attempts have been made to verify the information provided in this publication, neither the author nor the publisher assumes any responsibility for errors, omissions, or contrary interpretations of the subject matter herein. This book is for entertainment purposes only and should not be taken as expert instruction or commands. The Reader is responsible for his or her own actions.

Adherence to all applicable laws and regulations, including international federal, state, and local governing professional licensing, business practices, advertising and all other aspects of doing business in the US, Canada, or any other jurisdiction is the sole responsibility of the purchaser or reader. Neither the author nor the publisher assumes any responsibility or liability whatsoever on the behalf of the purchaser or reader of these materials.

365 DAYS OF THE WISEST THINGS EVER SAID— 1st Edition

Table of Contents

INTRODUCTION: QUOTES THAT CHANGE

Think about your favorite quote. What did it make you do? In this day and age, it's quite easy for one to forget how important quotes are to one's own self knowledge.

Furthermore, we often feel like we've heard enough quotes in our life. For example, one of my favorite quotes is "To be, or not to be, that is the question." This quote is great for so many reasons. For one, it has so many applications in the real world. From television shows to stand-up comedy acts to politics and governments, this particular quote can find a home. We often forget how such quotes can be applied in the everyday topics we think about.

In essence, the mind needs to constantly be filled with knowledge. Historical quotes are inherently filled with knowledge. We must accept quotes as an integral part of learning about the world around us. Many of the quotes found here may be one's that you have heard of, but many will be new.

How does a quote qualify as one of the wisest things ever said? It's based on change and behavior. There are at least two ways to read this book. One is my simply reading the quotes one-by-one. For example, the quote "Wherever you go, go with all your heart," by Confucius is quite compelling. Be passionate and make sure you are truly into what you're in to. Confucius believed happiness was attained by adopting certain behaviors and said so thousands of years ago. To this day, he continues to be a persevering influence in literature and world history. Many of the quotes here are just as compelling. After all, the individuals who said these quotes led influential lives. Thus, reading each quote by itself is effective and analyzing how it makes you feel is one way to read this book.

What does the word *inspiration* make you feel though? By definition, the word inspiration makes you feel mentally stimulated to have creative thoughts. Let me ask you another question: what feelings does the word *leadership* invoke? What about *life*? *Death*? How about the word *worldliness*? There's another way to read this book. Imagine we took the previously mentioned words such as inspiration, leadership, life, death, success, failure and worldliness and wrapped them in a process. I want you to do this three times with the quotes in this book. Reflect on this and then think about the possible circumstances they were in when they said the quotes that were attributed to them. How it relates to everything from life to death and the in-between. Following that, read the next quotes about success and failure. After all, life is filled with both. Think about the mistakes you see others make, then think about how others have succeeded in difficult situations.

You don't need to agree with every quote, but you do need to reflect on some of the wisest things ever said and how these quotes could change your outlook on the world. Many of these iconic individuals show up repeatedly and that's on purpose. By combining the quotes in a successive manner with the same iconic individuals repeatedly, you will know the circumstances the authors were living in and why quotes are more powerful together rather than alone.

365 QUOTES OF THE WISEST THINGS EVER SAID

He who possesses the source of enthusiasm will achieve great things. Doubt not. You will gather friends around you as a hair clasp gathers the hair.
—I Ching

INSPIRATION

Every man's life lies within the present; for the past is spent
and done with, and the future is uncertain.
—Marcus Aurelius

Friends are as companions on a journey, who ought to aid
each other to persevere in the road to a happier life.
—Pythagoras

Everything flows and nothing abides, everything gives way
and nothing stays fixed.
—Heraclitus

It is pleasurable, when winds disturb the waves of a great
sea, to gaze out from land upon the great trials of another
—Lucretius

Of all the things which wisdom provides to make us entirely happy, much the greatest is the possession of friendship.
—Epicurus

It is better to be full of drink than full of food.
—Hippocrates

Fall seven times and stand up eight
—Japanese Proverb

Everything comes gradually and at its appointed hour.
—Ovid

They are able because they think they are able.
—Virgil

Men, even when alone, lighten their labors by song, however

rude it may be.
—Marcus Fabius Quintilian

Every advantage in the past is judged in the light of the final issue.
—Demosthenes

If you wish to reach the highest, begin at the lowest.
—Publilius Syrus

Events will take their course, it is no good of being angry at them; he is happiest who wisely turns them to the best account.
—Euripides

Hold him alone truly fortunate who has ended his life in happy well-being.
—Aeschylus

History is philosophy teaching by example.
—Dionysius Periegetes

Freedom! Equality! Brotherhood!
—Motto

LEADERSHIP

Men of sense often learn from their enemies. It is from their foes, not their friends, that cities learn the lesson of building high walls and ships of war.
—Aristophanes

Everything that exists is in a manner the seed of that which will be.
—Marcus Aurelius

Fools take to themselves the respect that is given to their office.
—Aesop

If history is deprived of the Truth, we are left with nothing but an idle, unprofitable tale.
—Polybius

If there be light, then there is darkness; if cold, heat; if height, depth; if solid, fluid; if hard, soft; if rough, smooth; if calm, tempest; if prosperity, adversity; if life, death.
—Pythagoras

I have never wished to cater to the crowd; for what I know they do not approve, and what they approve I do not know.
—Epicurus

If you do not the expect the unexpected you will not find it, for it is not to be reached by search or trail.
—Heraclitus

In the midst of the fountain of wit there arises something bitter, which stings in the very flowers.
—Lucretius

To do the same thing over and over again is not only boredom: it is to be controlled by rather than to control what

you do.
—Heraclitus

Healing is a matter of time, but it is sometimes also a matter of opportunity.
—Hippocrates

I am a man, and whatever concerns humanity is of interest to me.
—Terence

Dripping water hollows out stone, not through force but through persistence.
—Ovid

Everything that has a beginning comes to an end.
—Marcus Fabius Quintilian

Few people can distinguish the genuinely good from the reverse.
—Juvenal

The easiest thing of all is to deceive one's self; for what a man wishes he generally believes to be true.
—Demosthenes

If our soldiers are not overburdened with money, it is not because they have a distaste for riches; if their lives are not unduly long, it is not because they are disinclined to longevity.
—Sun Tzu

I often regret that I have spoken; never that I have been silent.
—Publilius Syrus

Human misery must somewhere have a stop: there is no wind that always blows a storm.
—Euripides

In every tyrant's heart there springs in the end this poison, that he cannot trust a friend.
—Aeschylus

Manners make the person.
—Motto

LIFE AND DEATH (AND THE BETWEEN)

Your lost friends are not dead, but gone before, advanced a stage or two upon that road which you must travel in the steps they trod.
—Aristophanes

Despise not death, but welcome it, for nature wills it like all else.
—Marcus Aurelius

Appearances are deceptive.
—Aesop

How much better a thing it is to be envied than to be pitied.
—Herodotus

God is day and night, winter and summer, war and peace, surfeit and hunger.
—Heraclitus

If thou wilt make a man happy, add not unto his riches but take away from his desires.
—Epicurus

Nothing can be created out of nothing.
—Lucretius

There is nothing permanent except change.
—Heraclitus

Disease has a plurality of forms and a plurality of cures.
—Hippocrates

Far hence, keep far from me, you grim women!
—Ovid

The difficult is done at once,
the impossible takes a little longer.
—French Proverb

Forbidden pleasures alone are loved immoderately; when lawful, they do not excite desire.
—Marcus Fabius Quintilian

From where can your authority and license as a parent come from, when you who are old, do worse things?
—Juvenal

Fortune is like glass--the brighter the glitter, the more easily broken.
—Publilius Syrus

Forgive, son; men are men; they needs must err.
—Euripides

God is not averse to deceit in a holy cause.
—Aeschylus

Patiently bear the burden of poverty. [Lat., Paupertatis onus patienter ferre memento.]
—Dionysius Periegetes

Let us be tried by our actions.
—Motto

SUCCESS AND FAILURE

A man's homeland is wherever he prospers.
—Aristophanes

Rain does not fall on one roof alone.
—Cameroon Proverb

Dig within. Within is the wellspring of Good; and it is always
ready to bubble up, if you just dig.
—Marcus Aurelius

The measure of a man is the way he bears up under
misfortune.
—Plutarch

Little by little does the trick.
—Aesop

Illness strikes men when they are exposed to change.
—Herodotus

A society grows great when old men plant trees
whose shade they know they shall never sit in.
—Greek Proverb

Those who know how to win are much more numerous than
those who know how to make proper use of their victories.
—Polybius

Silence is better than unmeaning words.
—Pythagoras

Do not spoil what you have by desiring what you have not;
but remember that what you now have was once among the
things you only hoped for.
—Epicurus

Even sleepers are workers and collaborators on what goes
on in the universe.
—Heraclitus

Lovely it is, when the winds are churning up the waves on
the great sea, to gaze out from the land on the great efforts
of someone else.
—Lucretius

Everything in excess is opposed to nature.
—Hippocrates

I see the better things, and approve; I follow the worse.

—Ovid

Fear of the future is worse than one's present fortune.
—Marcus Fabius Quintilian

Even savage animals can agree among themselves.
—Juvenal

He who confers a favor should at once forget it, if he is not to show a sordid ungenerous spirit. To remind a man of a kindness conferred and to talk of it, is little different from reproach.
—Demosthenes

Do not despise the bottom rungs in the ascent to greatness.
—Publilius Syrus

Every man is like the company he is wont to keep.
—Euripides

Happiness is a choice that requires effort at times.
—Aeschylus

Ignorance of one's misfortunes is clear gain.
—Euripides

Necessity is stronger far than art.
—Aeschylus

Envy is honors foe.
—Motto

Listening to good advice is the way to wealth.
—Iranian Proverb

Memory is the treasure of the mind.
—English Proverb

Those who endure conquer.
—Motto

No man has a good enough memory to be a successful liar.
—Abraham Lincoln

All you need in this life is ignorance and confidence, and
then success is sure.
—Mark Twain

By three methods we may learn wisdom: First, by reflection,
which is noblest; Second, by imitation, which is easiest; and

third by experience, which is the bitterest.
—Confucius

It is the mark of an educated mind to be able to entertain a thought without accepting it.
—Aristotle

Words empty as the wind are best left unsaid.
—Homer

Everything that is made beautiful and fair and lovely is made for the eye of one who sees.
—Rumi

The man with insight enough to admit his limitations comes nearest to perfection.
—Johann Wolfgang von Goeth

The art of art, the glory of expression and the sunshine of the light of letters, is simplicity.
—Walt Whitman

Hope is the thing with feathers that perches in the soul - and sings the tunes without the words - and never stops at all.
—Emily Dickinson

People that seem so glorious are all show; underneath they are like everyone else.
—Euripides

To be rather than to seem.
—Aeschylus

Question everything. Learn something. Answer nothing.
—Motto

WORLDLINESS

Great effort is required to arrest decay and restore vigor. One must exercise proper deliberation, plan carefully before making a move, and be alert in guarding against relapse following a renaissance.
—I Ching

In union there is strength.
—Aesop

Great deeds are usually wrought at great risks.
—Herodotus

It is better wither to be silent, or to say things of more value than silence. Sooner throw a pearl at hazard than an idle or useless word; and do not say a little in many words, but a great deal in a few.
—Pythagoras

Fear was the first thing on earth to make gods
—Lucretius

It is convenient that there be gods, and, as it is convenient, let us believe that there are.
—Ovid

For it would have been better that man should have been born dumb, nay, void of all reason, rather than that he should employ the gifts of Providence to the destruction of his neighbor.
—Marcus Fabius Quintilian

Let thy speech be better than silence, or be silent.
—Dionysius of Halicarnassus

It is difficult not to write satire.
—Juvenal

From the errors of others a wise man corrects his own.
—Publilius Syrus

Do not plan for ventures before finishing what's at hand.
—Euripides

Eagles do not beget Doves.
—Motto

Wherever you go, go with all your heart.
—Confucius

Every day is a journey, and the journey itself is home.
—Matsuo Basho

The world is a book, and those who do not travel read only a page.
—Saint Augustine

The real voyage of discovery consists not in seeking new
landscapes, but in having new eyes.
—Marcel Proust

Unless what we do is useful, glory is vain.
—Latin Proverb

Words are mere bubbles of water,
but deeds are drops of gold.
—Chinese Proverb

It is better to travel well than to arrive.
—Buddha

A lie can travel halfway around the world while the truth is
putting on its shoes.
—Charles Spurgeon

A good traveler has no fixed plans, and is not intent on arriving.
—Lao Tzu

Like all great travellers, I have seen more than I remember, and remember more than I have seen.
—Benjamin Disraeli

We are what our thoughts have made us; so take care about what you think. Words are secondary. Thoughts live; they travel far.
—Swami Vivekananda

For once you have tasted flight you will walk the earth with your eyes turned skywards, for there you have been and there you will long to return.
—Leonardo da Vinci

We are all travelers in the wilderness of this world, and the best we can find in our travels is an honest friend.
—Robert Louis Stevenson

Though we travel the world over to find the beautiful, we must carry it with us or we find it not.
—Ralph Waldo Emerson

Rome is the city of echoes, the city of illusions, and the city of yearning.
—Giotto di Bondone

ACTIVITY I

Think about two or three behaviors you'd like to change. One of the best ways for humans to change a certain behavior is by finding champions they can follow to better themselves. Pick up to three champions from this section.

<u>Write what you like about them the most and how they can help motivate you to change those behaviors in the area below.</u>

INSPIRATIONAL v2

The responses of human beings vary greatly under dangerous circumstances. The strong man advances boldly to meet them head on. The weak man grows agitated. But the superior man stands up to fate, endures resolutely in his inner certainty If ignorant both.
—I Ching

He who lives in harmony with himself lives in harmony with the universe.
—Marcus Aurelius

In this theater of man's life, it is reserved only for God and angels to be lookers-on.
—Pythagoras

Greater dooms win greater destinies.
—Heraclitus

The greatest wealth is to live content with little, for there is never want where the mind is satisfied.
—Lucretius

Many admire, few know.
—Hippocrates

Fortune and love favor the brave.
—Ovid

Small opportunities are often the beginning of great
enterprises.
—Demosthenes

Learn to see in another's calamity the ills which you should
avoid.
—Publilius Syrus

Fortune truly helps those who are of good judgment.
—Euripides

Let nothing pass which will advantage you; Hairy in front,
Occasion's bald behind.
—Dionysius Periegetes

Freedom! Equality! Brotherhood!
—Motto

LEADERSHIP v2

The wise learn many things from their enemies.
—Aristophanes

Here is the rule to remember in the future, When anything tempts you to be bitter: not, "This is a misfortune" but "To bear this worthily is good fortune."
—Marcus Aurelius

It is easy to be brave when far away from danger.
—Aesop

In soft regions are born soft men.
—Herodotus

If God listened to the prayers of men, all men would quickly have perished: for they are forever praying for evil against one another.
—Epicurus

Idleness and lack of occupation tend - nay are dragged - towards evil.
—Hippocrates

Make the workmanship surpass the materials.
—Ovid

One thing, however, I must premise, that without the assistance of natural capacity, rules and precepts are of no efficacy.
—Marcus Fabius Quintilian

Like warmed-up cabbage served at each repast, The repetition kills the wretch at last.

—Juvenal

If you would live innocently, seek solitude.
—Publilius Syrus

I hate it in friends when they come too late to help.
—Euripides

It is easy when we are in prosperity to give advice to the afflicted.
—Aeschylus

Mercy is nobility's true badge.
—Motto

LIFE AND DEATH (AND THE BETWEEN) v2

Let me net it out for you, the pastor says as he concludes a sermon.
—Aristophanes

Each thing is of like form from everlasting and comes round again in its cycle.
—Marcus Aurelius

Beware lest you lose the substance by grasping at the shadow.
—Aesop

There is no witness so dreadful, no accuser so terrible as the conscience that dwells in the heart of every man.
—Polybius

It is impossible to live a pleasant life without living wisely and well and justly. And it is impossible to live wisely and well and justly without living a pleasant life.
—Epicurus

Pleasant it to behold great encounters of warfare arrayed over the plains, with no part of yours in peril.
—Lucretius

Hunger is alleviated by the drinking of neat wine.
—Hippocrates

He who is not prepared today will be less so tomorrow.
—Ovid

God, that all-powerful Creator of nature and architect of the world, has impressed man with no character so proper to

distinguish him from other animals, as by the faculty of
speech.
—Marcus Fabius Quintilian

Here we all live in a state of ambitious poverty.
—Juvenal

It is kindness to refuse immediately what you intend to deny.
—Publilius Syrus

God loves to help him who strives to help himself.
—Aeschylus

He is not a lover who does not love forever.
—Euripides

Married love between man and woman is bigger than oaths
guarded by right of nature.
—Aeschylus

Why should I fear death? If I am, death is not. If death is, I
am not. Why should I fear that which cannot exist when I do?
—Epicurus

Life asked death, 'Why do people love me but hate you?'
Death responded, 'Because you are a beautiful lie and I am
a painful truth.
—Unknown

Neither the sun, nor death can be looked at steadily.
—François de La Rochefoucauld

The boundaries which divide Life from Death are at best
shadowy and vague. Who shall say where the one ends, and
the other begins?

—Edgar Allan Poe

I do not fear death. I had been dead for billions and billions
of years before I was born, and had not suffered the slightest
inconvenience from it.
—Mark Twain

No one can confidently say that he will still be living
tomorrow.
—Euripides

To be fortunate is God, and more than God to mortals.
—Aeschylus

Safety is from God alone.
—Motto

SUCCESS AND FAILURE v2

Comedy is allied to justice.
—Aristophanes

Do every act of your life as if it were your last.
—Marcus Aurelius

Men often applaud an imitation and hiss the real thing.
—Aesop

The destiny of man is in his own soul.
—Herodotus

The most momentous thing in human life is the art of winning
the soul to good or evil.
—Pythagoras

I never desired to please the rabble. What pleased them, I did not learn; and what I knew was far removed from their understanding.
—Epicurus

Immortal mortals, mortal immortals, one living the others death and dying the others life.
—Heraclitus

Nothing is enough for the man to whom enough is too little.
—Epicurus

Behind every great man there's a great woman.
—American Proverb

Hard work is undesirable for the underfed.
—Hippocrates

Little things please little minds.
—Ovid

For comic writers charge Socrates with making the worse
appear the better reason.
—Marcus Fabius Quintilian

Every great house is full of haughty servants.
—Juvenal

Nothing is easier than self-deceit. For what each man
wishes, that he also believes to be true.
—Demosthenes

Everything is worth what its purchaser will pay for it.
—Publilius Syrus

I know how men in exile feed on dreams.
—Aeschylus

There is nothing like the sight of an old enemy down on his luck.
—Euripides

Impatience is the cause of most of our irregularities and extravagances Command by obeying.
—Motto

There are two ways of exerting one's strength: one is pushing down, the other is pulling up.
—Booker T. Washington

He who believes is strong; he who doubts is weak. Strong convictions precede great actions.
—Louisa May Alcott

Difficulties are meant to rouse, not discourage. The human spirit is to grow strong by conflict.
—William Ellery Channing

That which does not kill us makes us stronger.
—Friedrich Nietzsche

I love the man that can smile in trouble, that can gather strength from distress, and grow brave by reflection. 'Tis the business of little minds to shrink, but he whose heart is firm, and whose conscience approves his conduct, will pursue his principles unto death.
—Thomas Paine

True strength is keeping everything together when everyone
expects you to fall apart.
—Unknown

Always bear in mind that your own resolution to succeed is
more important than any other.
—Abraham Lincoln

If your actions inspire others to dream more, learn more, do
more and become more, you are a leader.
—John Quincy Adams

Without continual growth and progress, such words as
improvement, achievement, and success have no meaning.
—Benjamin Franklin

Take up one idea. Make that one idea your life - think of it, dream of it, live on that idea. Let the brain, muscles, nerves, every part of your body, be full of that idea, and just leave every other idea alone. This is the way to success.
—Swami Vivekananda

Success is not measured by what you accomplish, but by the opposition you have encountered, and the courage with which you have maintained the struggle against overwhelming odds.
—Orison Swett Marden

Before anything else, preparation is the key to success.
—Alexander Graham Bell

Discipline is the soul of an army. It makes small numbers formidable; procures success to the weak, and esteem to all.
—George Washington

There is nothing more difficult to take in hand, more perilous to conduct, or more uncertain in its success, than to take the lead in the introduction of a new order of things.
—Niccolo Machiavelli

Success is to be measured not so much by the position that one has reached in life as by the obstacles which he has overcome.
—Booker T. Washington

One should be of service rather than be conspicuous.
—Motto

If one advances confidently in the direction of his dreams, and endeavors to live the life which he has imagined, he will meet with a success unexpected in common hours.
—Henry David Thoreau

The battle of life is, in most cases, fought uphill; and to win it without a struggle were perhaps to win it without honor. If there were no difficulties there would be no success; if there were nothing to struggle for, there would be nothing to be achieved.
—Samuel Smiles

Invincibility lies in the defence; the possibility of victory in the attack.
—Sun Tzu

No man has a good enough memory to be a successful liar.
—Abraham Lincoln

My powers are ordinary. Only my application brings me success.
—Isaac Newton

Success or failure depends more upon attitude than upon capacity successful men act as though they have accomplished or are enjoying something. Soon it becomes a reality. Act, look, feel successful, conduct yourself accordingly, and you will be amazed at the positive results.
—William James

Whosoever desires constant success must change his conduct with the times.
—Niccolo Machiavelli

It had long since come to my attention that people of accomplishment rarely sat back and let things happen to them. They went out and happened to things.
—Leonardo da Vinci

Fortune befriends the bold.
—Emily Dickinson

If you are distressed by anything external, the pain is not due to the thing itself but to your own estimate of it; and this you have the power to revoke at any moment.
—Marcus Aurelius

Our insignificance is often the cause of our safety.
—Aesop

There are in fact two things, science and opinion; the former begets knowledge, the latter ignorance.
—Hippocrates

When it becomes more difficult to suffer than change -- then you will change.
—Unknown

WORLDLINESS v2

Little friends may prove great friends.
—Aesop

From the heart of the fountain of delight rises a jet of bitterness that tortures us among the very flowers.
—Lucretius

It is a wretched thing to live on the fame of others.
—Juvenal

It is a good thing to learn caution from the misfortunes of others.
—Publilius Syrus

It is change; all yields its place and goes.
—Euripides

Every accomplishment starts with the decision to try.
—Unknown

America will never be destroyed from the outside. If we falter and lose our freedoms, it will be because we destroyed ourselves.
—Abraham Lincoln

If the freedom of speech is taken away then dumb and silent we may be led, like sheep to the slaughter.
—George Washington

Man is free at the moment he wishes to be.
—Voltaire

The end of law is not to abolish or restrain, but to preserve and enlarge freedom. For in all the states of created beings capable of law, where there is no law, there is no freedom.
—John Locke

Our greatest happiness does not depend on the condition of life in which chance has placed us, but is always the result of a good conscience, good health, occupation, and freedom in all just pursuits.
—Thomas Jefferson

True individual freedom cannot exist without economic security and independence. People who are hungry and out of a job are the stuff of which dictatorships are made.
—Franklin D. Roosevelt

Without freedom of thought, there can be no such thing as wisdom - and no such thing as public liberty without freedom of speech.
—Benjamin Franklin

The cost of freedom is always high, but Americans have always paid it. And one path we shall never choose, and that is the path of surrender, or submission.
—John F. Kennedy

Freedom is never more than one generation away from extinction. We didn't pass it to our children in the bloodstream. It must be fought for, protected, and handed on for them to do the same.
—Ronald Reagan

It does not take a majority to prevail... but rather an irate, tireless minority, keen on setting brushfires of freedom in the minds of men.
—Samuel Adams

A lovely nook of forest scenery, or a grand rock, like a beautiful woman, depends for much of its attractiveness upon the attendance sense of freedom from whatever is low; upon a sense of purity and of romance.
—P. T. Barnum

It is difficult to free fools from the chains they revere.
—Voltaire

Americans are so enamored of equality that they would rather be equal in slavery than unequal in freedom.
—Alexis de Tocqueville

Americans are so enamored of equality that they would rather be equal in slavery than unequal in freedom.
—Alexis de Tocqueville

The rose speaks of love silently, in a language known only to the heart.
—Unknown

Nature always wears the colors of the spirit.
—Ralph Waldo Emerson

Keep close to Nature's heart... and break clear away, once in awhile, and climb a mountain or spend a week in the woods. Wash your spirit clean.
—John Muir

Every flower is a soul blossoming in nature.
—Gerard De Nerval

The day, water, sun, moon, night - I do not have to purchase these things with money.
—Plautus

Come forth into the light of things, let nature be your teacher.
—William Wordsworth

O, wind, if winter comes, can spring be far behind?
—Percy Bysshe Shelley

The natural liberty of man is to be free from any superior power on Earth, and not to be under the will or legislative authority of man, but only to have the law of nature for his rule.
—Samuel Adams

For my part I know nothing with any certainty, but the sight of the stars makes me dream.
—Vincent van Gogh

There is a certain enthusiasm in liberty, that makes human nature rise above itself, in acts of bravery and heroism.
—Alexander Hamilton

When virtue and modesty enlighten her charms, the lustre of a beautiful woman is brighter than the stars of heaven, and the influence of her power it is in vain to resist.
—Akhenaton

Let the beauty of what you love be what you do.
—Rumi

Great minds discuss ideas; average minds discuss events; small minds discuss people.
—Unknown

Everything has beauty, but not everyone sees it.
—Confucius

Education is the best friend. An educated person is respected everywhere. Education beats the beauty and the youth.
—Chanakya

The best part of beauty is that which no picture can express.
—Francis Bacon

I would define, in brief, the poetry of words as the rhythmical creation of Beauty.
—Edgar Allan Poe

Where justice is denied, where poverty is enforced, where ignorance prevails, and where any one class is made to feel that society is an organized conspiracy to oppress, rob and degrade them, neither persons nor property will be safe.
—Frederick Douglass

There is pleasure in the pathless woods, there is rapture in the lonely shore, there is society where none intrudes, by the deep sea, and music in its roar; I love not Man the less, but Nature more.
—Lord Byron

I think the first duty of society is justice.
—Alexander Hamilton

The reason why men enter into society is the preservation of their property.
—John Locke

To educate a man in mind and not in morals is to educate a menace to society.
—Theodore Roosevelt

If the same punishment is prescribed for two crimes that injure society in different degrees, then men will face no stronger deterrent from committing the greater crime if they find it in their advantage to do so.
—Cesare Beccaria

If religion has given birth to all that is essential in society, it is because the idea of society is the soul of religion.
—Émile Durkheim

No society can surely be flourishing and happy, of which the far greater part of the members are poor and miserable.
—Adam Smith

I had three chairs in my house; one for solitude, two for friendship, three for society.
—Henry David Thoreau

ACTIVITY II

Think about the different ways inspiration can manifest itself in your world. For example, in nature, the web, in thinking about possibilities, in people, and in yourself. Then, think about three things you always wanted to do.

Write down the three things you always wanted to do and how you're going to achieve it. Make a timeline for this year and make sure to act on it.

INSPIRATIONAL v3

It was a high counsel that I once heard given to a young person, always do what you are afraid to do.
—Ralph Waldo Emerson

The way of the creative works through change and transformation, so that each thing receives its true nature and destiny and comes into permanent accord with the great harmony: this is what furthers and what perseveres.
—I Ching

Nothing has such power to broaden the mind as the ability to investigate systematically and truly all that comes under thy observation in life.
—Marcus Aurelius

Rest satisfied with doing well, and leave others to talk of you as they will.
—Pythagoras

The sum of all sums is eternity.
—Lucretius

Natural forces within us are the true healers of disease.
—Hippocrates

Fortune resists half-hearted prayers.
—Ovid

No one knows what he can do until he tries.
—Publilius Syrus

Friends show their love in times of trouble…
—Euripides

A faithful companion is a sure anchor.
—Motto

A birthday is a good time to begin anew: throwing away the old habits, as you would old clothes, and never putting them on again.
—Bronson Alcott

Growth is the only evidence of life.
—John Henry Newman

If you're in a card game and you don't know who the suck is, you're it.
—Anonymous

At bottom every man knows well enough that he is a unique being, only once on this earth; and by no extraordinary chance will such a marvelously picturesque piece of diversity in unity as he is, ever be put together a second time.
—Friedrich Nietzsche

Where you find fault with something, come and give a hand.
—Estonian Proverb

No man is a hero to his own valet.
—Anonymous

Every cloud has a silver lining, every dog has his day.
—English Proverb

Keep your face always toward the sunshine—and shadows will fall behind you.
—Walt Whitman

It is always the simple that produces the marvelous.
—Amelia Edith Huddleston Barr

The glow of one warm thought is to me worth more than money.
—Thomas Jefferson

The power of imagination makes us infinite.
—John Muir

I believe that if one always looked at the skies, one would end up with wings.
—Gustave Flaubert

I dwell in possibility.
—Emily Dickinson

Light tomorrow with today.
—Elizabeth Barrett Browning

Happiness is a butterfly, which when pursued, is always just beyond your grasp, but which, if you will sit down quietly, may alight upon you.
—Nathaniel Hawthorne

LEADERSHIP v3

You cannot teach a crab to walk straight.
—Aristophanes

A faithful companion is a sure anchor.
—Motto

How much more grievous are the consequences of anger
than the causes of it.
—Marcus Aurelius

A spark can start a fire that burns the entire forest.
—Mongolia Proverb

Men who have lost heart have not yet won a trophy.
—Greek Proverb

Affairs are easier of entrance than of exit; and it is but
common prudence to see our way out before we venture in.
—Aesop

Neither snow, nor rain, nor heat, nor gloom of night stays these couriers from the swift completion of their appointed rounds.
—Herodotus

The time when most of you should withdraw into yourself is when you are forced to be in a crowd.
—Epicurus

Make a habit of two things: to help; or at least to do no harm.
—Hippocrates

Those who wish to appear wise among fools, among the wise seem foolish.
—Marcus Fabius Quintilian

Many individuals have, like uncut diamonds, shining qualities beneath a rough exterior.
—Juvenal

To confess a fault freely is the next thing to being innocent of
it.
—Publilius Syrus

Impudence is the worst of all human diseases.
—Euripides

The man whose authority is recent is always stern.
—Aeschylus

The wealth of kings is in the affections of their subjects.
—Motto

LIFE AND DEATH (AND THE BETWEEN) v3

Quickly, bring me a beaker of wine, so that I may wet my mind and say something clever.
—Aristophanes

Let men see, let them know, a real man, who lives as he was
meant to live.
—Marcus Aurelius

The little reed, bending to the force of the wind, soon stood
upright again when the storm had passed over.
—Aesop

Do not eat your heart.
—Pythagoras

It is possible to provide security against other ills, but as far
as death is concerned, we men all live in a city without walls.
—Epicurus

Life is short, science is long; opportunity is elusive,
experiment is dangerous, judgement is difficult.
—Hippocrates

Time the devourer of everything.
—Ovid

Our minds are like our stomaches; they are whetted by the change of their food, and variety supplies both with fresh appetite.
—Marcus Fabius Quintilian

Now we suffer the evils of a long peace; luxury more cruel than war broods over us and avenges a conquered world.
—Juvenal

Life itself is short, but lasts longer than misfortunes.
—Publilius Syrus

Beauty without virtue is like a rose without scent.

—Swedish Proverb

The best prophet is common sense, our native wit.
—Euripides

Nearly all men can stand adversity, but if you want to test a
man's character, give him power.
—Abraham Lincoln

This above all: to thine own self be true,
And it must follow, as the night the day,
Thou canst not then be false to any man.
—William Shakespeare

It is in the thirties that we want friends. In the forties we know
they won't save us any more than love did.
—Euripides

Call no man happy till he is dead.
—Aeschylus

One can survive everything nowadays, except death, and live down anything, except a good reputation.
—Oscar Wilde

When someone you love becomes a memory, the memory becomes a treasure
—Unknown

When the game is over, the king and the pawn go into the same box.
—Italian Proverb

Naked a man comes from his mother's womb, and as he comes, so he departs. He takes nothing from his labor that he can carry in his hand.
—King Solomon

Because I could not stop for Death, He kindly stopped for me. The Carriage held but just ourselves And Immortality.
—Emily Dickinson

Tis very certain the desire of life prolongs it.
—Lord Byron

While I thought that I was learning how to live, I have been learning how to die.
—Leonardo da Vinci

Death may be the greatest of all human blessings.
—Socrates

Death never takes the wise man by surprise; He is always ready to go.
—Jean de La Fontaine

Death is a delightful hiding place for weary men.
—Herodotus

We understand death for the first time when he puts his hand upon one whom we love.
—Madame de Stael

I had friends. The idea of being forever separated from them and from all their troubles is one of the greatest sorrows that I suffer in dying. Let them at least know that to my latest moment I thought of them.
—Marie Antoinette

Death is better, a milder fate than tyranny.
—Aeschylus

For certain is death for the born
And certain is birth for the dead;
Therefore over the inevitable
Thou shouldst not grieve.
—Bhagavad Gita

SUCCESS AND FAILURE v3

If you are distressed by anything external, the pain is not due to the thing itself but to your own estimate of it; and this you have the power to revoke at any moment.
—Marcus Aurelius

The injuries we do and the injuries we suffer are seldom weighed on the same scales.
—Aesop

Man's character is his fate.
—Heraclitus

The misfortune of the wise is better than the prosperity of the fool.
—Epicurus

Plenty has made me poor.
—Ovid

Though ambition in itself is a vice, yet it is often the parent of virtues.
—Marcus Fabius Quintilian

Many commit the same crime with a different destiny; one bears a cross as the price of his villainy, another wears a crown.
—Juvenal

There is a great deal of wishful thinking in such cases; it is the easiest thing of all to deceive one's self.
—Demosthenes

Familiarity breeds contempt.
—Publilius Syrus

It is always in season for old men to learn.
—Aeschylus

The wavering mind is but a base possession.
—Euripides

Mighty in deeds and not in words.
—Motto

Let not your mind run on what you lack as much as on what you have already.
—Marcus Aurelius

No act of kindness, no matter how small, is ever wasted.
—Aesop

The art of living well and the art of dying well are one.
—Epicurus

The life so short, the craft so long to learn.
—Hippocrates

Vision without action is daydream.
Action without vision is nightmare.
—Japanese Proverb

WORLDLINESS v3

Many receive advice, only the wise profit from it.
—Publilius Syrus

A man who cannot tolerate small ills
can never accomplish great things.
—Chinese Proverb

The majority of men are bundles of beginnings.
—Ralph Waldo Emerson

Contemplate thy powers, contemplate thy wants, and thy
connections; so shalt thou discover the duties of life, and be
directed in all thy ways.
—Akhenaton

The childhood shows the man, as morning shows the day.
—John Milton

Who does not grow, declines.
—Rabbi Hillel

I have always found that mercy bears richer fruits than strict justice.
—Abraham Lincoln

Courage is of no value unless accompanied by justice; yet if all men became just, there would be no need for courage.
—Agesilaus the Second

The sword of justice has no scabbard.
—Antione De Riveral

In the state of nature, indeed, all men are born equal, but they cannot continue in this equality. Society makes them lose it, and they recover it only by the protection of the laws.
—Charles de Montesquieu

Society cannot exist unless a controlling power upon will and appetite be placed somewhere, and the less of it there is within, the more there must be without.
—Edmund Burke

As one grows older, one becomes wiser and more foolish.
—François de La Rochefoucauld

Wisdom is not finally tested in the schools, Wisdom cannot be pass'd from one having it to another not having it, Wisdom is of the soul, is not susceptible of proof, is its own proof.
—Walt Whitman

Don't go around saying the world owes you a living. The world owes you nothing. It was here first.
—Mark Twain

Time is at once the most valuable and the most perishable of all our possessions.
—John Randolph

All truths are easy to understand once they are discovered; the point is to discover them.
—Galileo Galilei

I do not know what I may appear to the world; but to myself I seem to have been only like a boy playing on the seashore, and diverting myself in now and then finding a smoother pebble or a prettier shell than ordinary, whilst the great ocean of truth lay all undiscovered before me.
—Isaac Newton

Without perseverance talent is a barren bed.
—Welsh Proverb

ACTIVITY III

Think about five ways you displayed leadership in the past. What did you do right and what did you do wrong? What kind of leader are you?

Write how you motivated others in the past and led them to success. Also acknowledge the times you failed to bring the best resolution to these situations. Record these and write what you will do in the future to be the best leader you can be to others.

SELECTED QUOTED SOURCES

Abraham Lincoln (1809–1865), 16th President of the United States

Adam Smith (1723–1790), Pioneer of Political Economy

Aeschylus (545–456 BC), Tragedian

Aesop (620 BC–564 BC), Greek Fabulist

Agesilaus the Second (444–360 BC), Spartan King

Akhenaton (1380–1334 BC), Egyptian Pharaoh

Alexander Hamilton (1757–1804), 1st United States Secretary of the Treasury

Alexis de Tocqueville (1805–1859), 19th Century French Political Scientist

Amelia Edith Huddleston Barr (1831–1919), British Novelist

Antione De Riveral (1753–1801), Royalist French Writer"

Aristophanes (445–385 BC), Greek Comic

Benjamin Disraeli (1804–1881), The Earl of Beaconsfield

Benjamin Franklin (1706–1790), Renowned Polymath

Bhagavad Gita (200 BC), A Sanskrit Epic

Booker T. Washington (1856–1915), American Educator

Bronson Alcott (1799–1888), Member of the Transcendental Club

Cesare Beccaria (1738–1794), Italian Criminologist

Chanakya (371–283 BC), Royal Advisor

Charles de Montesquieu (1689–1755), Lawyer of the Age of Enlightenment

Confucius (551–479 BC), Chinese Philosophy

Demosthenes (384–322 BC), Greek Statesman

Dionysius of Halicarnassus (60– after 7 BC), Greek Historian

Dionysius Periegetes (Unknown Dates), The Traveller

Edgar Allan Poe (1809–1849), American Poet

Edmund Burke (1729–1797), Irish Statesman

Elizabeth Barrett Browning (1806–1861), Victorian Poet

Émile Durkheim (1858–1917), Father of Sociology

Emily Dickinson (1830–1886), American Poet

Epicurus (341–270 BC), Greek Philosopher

Euripides (480–406 BC), Greek Tragedian

Francis Bacon (1561–1626), Lord Chancellor of England

François de La Rochefoucauld (1613–1680), French Writer

Franklin D. Roosevelt (1882–1945), 32nd President of the United States

Frederick Douglass (1818–1895), American Abolitionist

Friedrich Nietzsche (1844–1900), German Philologist

Galileo Galilei (1564–1642), Italian Polymath

George Washington (1732–1799), 1st President of the United States

Gerard De Nerval (1808–1855), French Essayist

Giotto di Bondone (1266–1337), Renaissance Architect

Gustave Flaubert (1821–1880), Leader of Literary Realism

Henry David Thoreau (1817–1862), American Essayist

Heraclitus (535–475 BC), Greek Philosopher

Herodotus (484–425 BC), Greek Historian

Hippocrates (460–370 BC), Greek Physician

I Ching (Between 10th and 4th centuries BC), Ancient Chinese Text

Isaac Newton (1643–1727), English Physicist

Jean de La Fontaine (1621–1695), French Fabulist

John F. Kennedy (1917–1963), 32nd President of the United States

John Henry Newman (1801–1890), English Theologian

John Locke (1632–1704), English Philosopher

John Milton (1608–1674), English Poet
John Muir (1838–1914), American Naturalist
John Quincy Adams (1767–1848), 6th President of the United States
John Randolph (1773–1833), American Congressman
Juvenal (Unknown Dates), Roman Poet
King Solomon (Unknown Dates), King of Israel
Lao Tzu (605–531 BC), Chinese Philosopher
Leonardo da Vinci (1452–1519), Italian Polymath
Lord Byron (1788–1824), Leader of the Romantic Movement
Louisa May Alcott (1832–1888), American Novelist
Lucretius (99–55 BC), Roman Poet
Madame de Stael (1766–1817), Woman of Jetters
Marcel Proust (1871–1922), French Novelist
Marcus Aurelius (121–180), Roman Emperor
Marcus Fabius Quintilian (35–100), Roman Rhetorician
Mark Twain (1835–1910), American Writer
Matsuo Basho (1644–1694), Japanese Poet
Nathaniel Hawthorne (1804–1864), American Short Story Writer
Niccolo Machiavelli (1469–1527), Founder of Modern Political Science
Orison Swett Marden (1850–1924), American Inspirational Author
Ovid (43 BC–17 AD), Roman Poet
P. T. Barnum (1810–1891), Founder of Barnum and Bailey Circus
Plutarch (45–120), Greek Biographer
Polybius (264–146 BC), Greek Historian
Publilius Syrus (85–43 BC), Latin Writer
Pythagoras (570–495), Ionian Greek Philosopher

Ralph Waldo Emerson (1803–1882), American Essayist
Robert Louis Stevenson (1850–1894), Scottish Novelist
Ronald Reagan (1911–2004), 40th President of the United States
Saint Augustine (354–430), Bishop of Hippo Regius
Samuel Smiles (1812–1904), Scottish Author
Sun Tzu (544–496 BC), Chinese General
Swami Vivekananda (1863–1902), Hindu Monk
Terence (186–159 BC), Roman Playwright
Theodore Roosevelt (1858–1919), 26th President of the United States
Thomas Jefferson (1743–1826), 3rd President of the United States
Thomas Paine (1737–1809), American Revolutionary
Vincent van Gogh (1853–1890), Dutcher Painter
Virgil (70–19 BC), Roman Poet
Voltaire (1694–1778), French Enlightenment Writer
Walt Whitman (1819–1892), American Poet
William Ellery Channing (1780–1842), Unitarian Preacher
William James (1842–1910), American Philosopher

A MODEST REQUEST

Hello! Did you like the book? I want to say thanks for taking the time to go through this book. There's plenty of books on quotations out there, but you decided to give me a chance!

If I may ask one favor, would you be able to leave a review for this book? Does not have to be long. It could as little as one sentence.

Reviews are one of the best ways to thank authors and I appreciate it very much.

Thanks for your time,

Max Winters

Made in the USA
Coppell, TX
27 November 2021

66537868R00062